prime meridian

POEMS BY
CONNIE POST

GLASS LYRE PRESS

Copyright © 2020 Connie Post
Paperback ISBN: 978-1-941783-66-5

All rights reserved: Except for the purpose of quoting brief passages for review, no part of this book may be reproduced or transmitted in any form or by any means, electronic or mechanical, including photocopying, recording, or by any information storage and retrieval system, without permission in writing from the publisher.

Design & Layout: Steven Asmussen
Cover Art: Tracy McQueen
Copyediting: Linda E. Kim

Glass Lyre Press, LLC
P.O. Box 2693
Glenview, IL 60025
www.GlassLyrePress.com

PRIME MERIDIAN

*For Kevin, love of my life,
and keeper of my heart*

Contents

Fault Lines	1
Crumbling	2
Hula Hoop Turns 50	3
Accessory After the Fact	5
Four Miles from the Center of Town	6
After Winter	7
Walking Beside October	8
Feast	9
Sunday in September	10
When I Was in Grade School	11
Gardening	12
Solstice	13
Catatonic Walk While the Sun Drops Out of the Sky	14
Shadow Light	15
Give it Back	16
MRI	17
Flash Flood	18
Forgotten War	19
Shading	20
De-boning a Fish	21
Burn	22
Silences	23
Curvature of the Spine	24
Sister's Choral Concert 1978	25
Daily Worship	26
Iron Will	27
Lent	28
Prime Meridian	29
Aisle Five, Sheets and Linens	30
How to Sort the Living from the Dead	31

The Night Before Surgery	32
Tempur-pedic	33
Fragments	34
The Day Breaks Off in Uneven Chunks	35
Rupture	36
To Someone I Must Forget	37
Living Abroad	38
1976 YouTube of Nadia Comaneci	39
Travel Guide	40
Exit Here	41
When in Doubt	42
Vacant	43
Fade In	44
Back Stage	45
It's No Secret	46
Thursday Night Walk With the Dog	47
Taking a Walk on the Path Behind Our House	48
All this Talk	49
Ornithology	50
Raven in Flight	51
As the Week Goes By	52
The Burial was Wednesday	53
Looking for the Father's name	54
For All of Us Who	55
Coastal College Town	56
How to Watch a Bird Die	57
Infatuation	58
Strands	59
Become	60
Omen	61

Acknowledgments 63
About the Author 67

Fault Lines

A small earthquake
is reported
fifty plus miles
from where you live

you wonder if that explains why
you tripped last night
while meandering in your sleep

it's morning
you go to the kitchen
drink dark coffee
and pet the dog

as the day rolls by
you think about a geologist
crossing a room
quickly studying spikes and patterns
finding a way
to give a numerical value
to the earth's unsettled self

4.2 has its own meaning.
magnitude, years
centuries

as evening descends
you look up facts
about tectonic plates
and oceanic crusts

you haven't spoken to your family
in fifteen years

you wonder how much longer
a fault line
can maintain its own silence

Crumbling

Mountains

civilizations

houses

each succumbs
to a kind of gravity
a weight which
they can no longer bear

I hear my ceiling
creak
with everything you ever said
that made the walls emaciated

I watch the women
in my family
recede into themselves
like a once prosperous village

hiding now in the huts
that were made for them
after a long war

every night I hear
a distant thunder
and a broken sky

each time
the roof over my head
seems a little thinner

but I hold this gravity
like a prayer in my hands

making sure it stays
close to me

until the next time
my bones decide
to speak the language
of falling stones

Hula Hoop Turns 50
– Associated Press June 19, 2008

In 1967, there were few things
I wanted more than my own
cylindrical, smooth, plastic
neon pink hoop

like a story,
I climbed inside the sphere
again and again
when my waist was still straight and bony

countless times, I dropped it to the back patio
the scratches around the rim, always appeared
after the first few days of summer

I never understood the "shoop shoop" noise
what places of the earth were inside it,
but it must have been deepest black —
I believed it had something to do
with the reason my father walked towards me
so often
watching intently, the motion of my hips
teaching my body to understand
the irrevocable forces of gravity

each week, I learned better
how to navigate my own talents —
I already knew I was a sinner
as mother told me at night
for not saying my prayers

but I knew (better than she) what was more important —
I practiced all the time
I was bonded to the idea of retrieval
how the hoop would drop below my knees
spiral downward
how desperately
I needed to predict descent

the summers passed
the patio covering crumbled in unpredictable patterns
eventually, I started practicing in the side yard,
but he found me anyway

I forgot how to pray
but each day, I would rehearse —
understanding better each time
the undulations of a broken dance

the sound of the death rattle

Accessory After the Fact

I destroy the evidence
upon waking
wash the blood
from bad dreams

I make sure there is no
subconscious spatter
on the curtains
or floor
the blankets are pulled
from the bed
washed over and over

I cover the mattress
with a loose sheet
hide the evidence
— the shards of night
I hope nobody notices
how I left my body
fled the crime scene

burned the dreams
with one lit match
the ashes of a single nocturne
falling out of my mouth

Four Miles from the Center of Town

You will find the body
at the far side of the field
past the sagging rocks
beyond the milk thistle weeds
and the crippled crows

you will need a dog
—who only responds
to sign language

you will need to search
only in fall
when the dusk
smothers the trees

you will need a rope
so you can tie yourself
to a large boulder
when the
soil caves in

you will need a small camera
so you can remember yourself
standing there in
the smoldering light

you will find
the sallow, bent body
the smaller self
you
the barely thirteen-year-old
girl lying lifeless
pretending no one will find her
learning to live
in the shallow grave of silence

After Winter

The ground water
is contaminated
the birds are dying
for unknown reasons

the moon is choking
—the equator is bent

the ozone layer
swallows
its own tongue

the storm drains
fill with acid rain

and the small invisible girl
with the small porcelain doll
is falling backwards

and all she can do
is drink the water
she was given

find the boy
who said he wanted
to be a cartographer
when he grows up

and begin unfolding
his bruised hands

Walking Beside October

I come across a blue grey salamander
frozen
in the middle of the wooden bridge

I step over it
and it thanks me
by scurrying away

I think of the way
I used to
stop in the hallway
when you'd pass
hoping you would not
spill your Jack Daniels
down my legs
hoping your shirt buttons
were fastened

I remind myself why
I take walks at dusk
when the sunlight
abandons the house

I hear solstice
calling me home

I hear the salamander
move the weeds aside
and run back
to the shallow creek bed

I look back
and thank this traveler
of this small country
for teaching me
how move across a rugged terrain
without a passport
or even a name

Feast

There will be two meals
served at the dinner table tonight

the one with the teal blue place settings
where the cracked shadows reside

the one you will spoon feed
to your mother who has already died

the place where the tablecloth is creased
just so — where scorn hides

the legs of the table will shudder
as if the mahogany
were memory

the glasses will clank in unison
at the table
even when
there is no earthquake

when everyone has gone
to the porch
you will finally
tend to the second meal

the one you will feed
to the rabid dog
under the table

the same one
you kill each night
before the dream ends

Sunday in September

I saw you exiting the grocery store today
It's been over twenty years
since we've spoken
but I still see you now and again

I think this time
you recognized me first
but this time,
I was the one who made you look away
you, whom I used to call Father

at the other end of the parking lot
six police cars barricade the entrance
arresting some guy
who stole a basket of groceries
the siren lights
unmistakably quiet and measured

I watched you get into your car
a slightly hunched over
old man
holding two half filled
bags of groceries

a Korean war veteran
rapist of children
driving away
in an old silver Buick

the police
reading Miranda rights
to someone else

while I watch you drive away

When I Was in Grade School

My father used to say
"I can snap your arm like a twig"

I went outside
every day
spending more time with the trees

learned the language of the bark
while unfolding myself under the shade

I went on long walks
collected broken branches
and garbage
from the roadside

I tripped over tree roots
sticking out like bone
from beneath the earth's skin

as the years went by
I built a hidden tree house

there are no doors
just quiet places
to enter and exit

Gardening

After my father
would beat one of us
he would place flowers
on the kitchen table
the next morning

he cut the stems flush
and laid the begonias in a circle
in an inch of water

the lavender and fuchsia
permeated the morning

we were called to breakfast
we ate waffles
and said nothing of the raging blooms

the apologies
buried in the ordered way
the flowers were arranged

we looked down at our plates
eating
eating
gorging
ignoring his
sun scorched hands

these days
I spend time
pulling petals
out of my body

placing a shovel
in the open earth
placing flowers
back into the ground

Solstice

There are cemeteries
off the main road
of the body

clusters of tombstones beneath the skin
a swollen spot on the back of your neck

there are dates engraved
in the shallow
spaces beneath your rib cage

you bring orchids to a clearing
in the slivered grass
you kneel when no one is looking

you unfold your hands
—wonder how the Eucalyptus
grew so tall — so fast
how your bones bend
with gale force winds

as you turn away
from your salt bone self
distant cars pass by
people point and wonder
about the gravel path
etched
beyond your calcified spine

you don't hear the cars
all you hear are the
grave diggers
coming towards you
begging you to unhinge
your mouth

imploring you
to pull out each grief
place each quietly
on the stones
with no name

Catatonic Walk While the Sun Drops Out of the Sky

End of summer

end of the moon

end of the prophecies

end of all of the dreams of Armageddon
you've ever had

end of the sidewalk

end of the muddy river

end of all the deities
you ever wondered about

I watch you regurgitate
your life
as if it will go on and on

I choke on mine
and hope it will pass through me

I tug the end of this rope
hanging from this old metal bridge

and slide down the embankment
into the water

I know you cannot forgive me
or the soil
for how calm we are
when we slide to the bottom
of this exalted river

Shadow Light

It seems normal
when I close the curtains
like anguish

the dawn
crushes the fig trees
standing like naked bodies
outside my window

I stretch myself
carefully
across the hallway
but autumn
does not understand mercy

I find a glass of water
on the kitchen counter
I don't know why I left it there
last night

there are molecules
of tranquil intelligence
hydrogen, oxygen
that find themselves
in the spillway of my throat

the tiny stones from my ears
fall inward
—a divination of my
own body's equator

they pass through me
like a labor
prolonged
protracted
like some
ordinary truth

Give it Back

I ask the night
to give back
all the sleep it has taken
from me

but it laughs at me
as if I am a peasant
approaching the leader
of an oppressed country

I will not grovel
in the gray of dusk
I will not pray
for morning

I will wade through
the layers of dawn
as if it is murky water
that leads me out of a dungeon

and when all of the soldiers of mourning
line up to meet me

I will salute them in silence
drop to my knees
kiss the ground
as if it's the first time
I have traveled to this
foreign land

MRI

Sliding inside
the long narrow tube
is like sliding back
into my mother's womb

the air circulates
like amniotic fluid
thick
heavy
waiting for release

I remember nothing
of the life I had before
forget how bones calcify —
how a spine bends
to the world's suffering

I don't remember
who brought me here

I only remember
this tunnel
— the way edges disappear

I don't understand
the cathedrals inside
a body

I only know how to
find my way out

when no one else
is looking

Flash Flood

Like dread
in a storm drain
you rise in my throat

I choke on warm rain

I wonder
if this is what drowning
feels like

but there is no struggle
no frantic hand movements
no sputtering
or swallowed words

I find my way
to the surface
only to see you
standing on the sidewalk
silent now
watching
our last conversation
pool near the gutter

acting as if
all these sand bags
you carried here
will make a difference

when all the levees are broken

Forgotten War

You stumbled around the house
through most of the 1970's
sometimes muttering things
about young Korean girls
I didn't understand

you took long fishing trips
to the dark water
and wouldn't return until
there was no breath left in that lake

I asked mom about it once —
I knew you had been in a war
but didn't understand
it had anything to do
with your off-center gait
the rage you held in your right shoulder,
the passing out at seven p.m. on the couch

one day, I went to get a popsicle
in the garage refrigerator
and you were standing there
one hand as always on the Pabst Blue Ribbon
and I asked
"did you ever kill anyone in the war"
you went silent, looked away

but I knew already
I knew it in the way you laid
the hooked fish on the counter
the way you cut one long line
down each body
severing their forgiven skins

taking the eyes out,
saying they were a delicacy
in other countries
you seeing in me, how relieved I was
they could not see you anymore

I knew the lake would someday disavow the fish
as I have you
but at times when I drive past a murky lake
I still see us, stumbling over the Seoul soaked fields
of our forgotten war

Shading

I am standing in a
vacant room

I am blending the light
as if it were watercolor

I try the shadow light
mixed with fading light
—it makes me remember how
a life recedes

I cannot get the backdrop
exactly right
so I throw in some slanted light
and later —slats of hallway light

I want a sky that shocks
the viewer
so I texture in the fierce light
that has forced you
to automatically
swallow your own
darkness

if light could break open
it would remember how
you mixed yourself
beyond recognition

De-boning a Fish

I wonder what the fish
saw in my father
before he gutted them

were they relieved
to know
they'd soon be out of misery

relieved
to stop gasping for air,
to cease
the futile flailing around
the counter top

did they wait
within themselves
and pray for the
long knife

did they remember the lake
its muddy bottom,
knowing they can never return

you can tell me
(and I already know)
that fish
don't understand
these kinds of things

but neither does
a small child

at some point
don't we all beg
for mercy

Burn

I have been on fire
since the moment I walked
through this door

the ashen gray walls
are smoldering

there is molten lava
coming out of your mouth
words sliding
down the mountain side
of your throat

I enter the crematorium
of your mind
understanding
how a thought ignites

I never know what to do
when you give them back
contained
yet
formless

I leave the room
stand at the end of the hallway
holding urns of conversations

trying to remember
the bone yards of our beginnings

the decades
that we lived in the same house
the matches hidden
in all the closets
we never opened

those we never will

Silences

You fear the short silences
the small slots you fall through

you tip toe across the muted paths
of conversation
as if nothing matters

you try to keep up —
say things that make you sound
— comfortable

but secretly
you dread the severed silences
watching your own words fall from a cliff
and drown in their own blood

you prefer the long eloquent silence
of a tango

the long languid ledge
of a wordless day

you wait patiently on the veranda
to hold hands
with the cool side of midnight

you tap your foot
on the stony edge of night
until the earth stops breathing
so you can finally reveal
your forked tongue
and call out
in a century that is not your own
and hope someone hears you

Curvature of the Spine
(Sister, One Year Older Than Me)

I watched the doctors
trace lines down your back
with an index finger
I watched you bend over,
time and time again
touch the barren floor
as they measured the curve,
the stubborn spine
the radiologist telling mom
what to expect
reminding us, how a body
makes up its mind

the heavy radiation aprons
falling from your thin body
your pelvic bones, off center

after each check up,
I grasped my own bones at night
making sure they weren't winding
out of control

the years passed,
the hair brush beatings got worse,
the scoliosis followed you to high school —
the awkward braces
the tightening of the bodice around the ribs
how you already understood
the language of shallow breath

the only time you were allowed
to take off the brace, was bed time.
I watched you unlace each strap
the sores from abrasion, the pulling
spoke like ancient rubbings from a cave wall
I never said a thing
as you snuck quietly into the bed next to me
you always turned off the lamp first

I waited for night to be over, for contrition
I waited
until I heard your steady, full breath
as if you already knew our survival
was curving into itself

Sister's Choral Concert 1978

She is in the second row from the bottom
the first song after intermission erupts
and I pretend to listen

I pretend to care about singing
she tells me she is in A cappella
all it means to me is that I can
hear the collective breath of the choir
between the coda

I watched her mouth move
I could not tell which sound was hers
but I studied the silent "o" of her lips
the way each word was a stone
falling off a sheer cliff

I studied the movement
the kinesiology of lost sound

I resented her half-parted lips
I wished she understood
the narrow chamber of silence

it felt almost the same
when our father entered our
bedrooms at night

how the half notes
bent themselves inside
the un-noticed parts of the closet

how the whole notes
spilled backwards
into a motherless hallway

Daily Worship

Sometimes a mother is a prayer
an altar upon which your knees break

the stones rumble
like old family friends
who refuse to believe a word you say

each story you repeat
is more like a psalm
you were forced to memorize
in catholic school

each lie falls out of your mouth
like something you know
you are supposed to say
when the priest
marks your forehead with ashes

you forget
how you took too much holy water
during the sign of the cross
before Sunday Mass

you find yourself kneeling
in the middle of empty streets
your knees bruised again
wearing a thin, acrid cloak

your mother
just around the corner
screaming at you
from the steps of the same church
the confessionals crumbling
behind her

the cathedral folding into itself

the sky
a burning sacrament

Iron Will

When the years were lean
my mother
ironed the clothing of others
to make ends meet

she pressed through the day
when my father was gone
working two jobs

I watched her
smooth the history
out of each rumpled seam

as the steam rose
from the fabric
I understood how
precision
lives the quiet life of rage

I asked her often
"when are you going to be done"
but she never answered

the days bled into years
of beatings
followed by the imperative séance of silence

I left home young
my car full of short skirts and wrinkled blouses

as the decades passed
I turned away

but sometimes
I still see her, standing there
fastening a floral apron
tripping on the cord of her own life
rising
falling
putting garments back on their hangers
adjusting the collars
following the crease lines
just so

Lent

I am giving up breathing
for lent

it should be easy
my rib cage
has been begging me for a rest

my lungs are collapsing
at the weight
of dirty penance

my throat can go quiet now
say its last prayer

there are forty days
I will go un-noticed
forty doctors who will call
time of death

forty death certificates
hand written in the salt of earth
each will give a different reason
for my demise

and at the end of the season
I will stand at the hallway
of this broken church
and pretend
I am no longer hungry

Prime Meridian

Step upon the earth
as if it is melting

fold the continents
as if the borders
were already singed
at the edges

hold a container
and let all of the oceans run
inside of it
drink the salt
until it is all that's left of us

succumb to the talons
of the last orphaned eagle
let it pull you up by your shirt collar
and sail you across
the life you were supposed to have

look down
and watch the glaciers fall
the oceans rise
the inlets of every river
drown inside themselves

listen for
the sound of your own voice
falling backwards

listen for the sound
of the ocean turning itself under

as if the earth were a womb
and you the child
passing through

Aisle Five, Sheets and Linens

I am looking for the flattest, darkest one
hoping it will cover me, at a moment's notice

I wonder if the thousand thread count
will shield me
from the coarse night

if I keep the ends un-tucked
will the shadows in the room
find a way to creep up my legs,
after the light has been folded back

I stand in this aisle,
imagining my bed collapse again
under the weight of its own knowledge

I wonder
how many times
I can strip this mattress of its membranes
how many times
I can pretend
there is a way to cover
the indents of regret

How to Sort the Living from the Dead

Forget all the nonsense
about eyes opened or closed
or breathing
or brain waves

ignore the sallow skin
the pulse
or even the way
they stare back at you

find the place
where the hands
are swollen with regret

find the place where
silence is the chest bone

find the dental imprints
of a life not eaten

find the eulogy
that is transfixed
in your dust bound bones

find the small minutes
where each of us
wander through
a fractured room

remember how to
immerse your amnesia
in embalming fluid

teach yourself
how to leave a body
and then
how to return

The Night Before Surgery

Take the dog
on a long walk

the one where you pass
the old metal bridge
beyond the area
marked "mud slide"

watch his footsteps carefully
and he will help you
find the places
to hide
when you
enter that long
languid
journey of anesthesia

watch the way
his fur mingles
with the slight breeze
how he follows the faint edges
of a gravel path

feel the cadence
the rise and fall of his lungs
and tell him
you will see him there
on the ledge of solitude
and remember
he will teach you
everything about the anaphora
that stays in the body
that stays beneath your skin
as apparent
as faded scar tissue
or mercy

Tempur-pedic

The salesman tells me
"it molds to the contours of your body"

he smiles
and I feel the disks in my back
give way

"memory foam is the best thing
for you"

I stare past him
realize he has never spent a night
parked in bones like mine

never folded himself
in the sway back of a hammock
felt his joints fall
towards the sparse grass below

he doesn't understand
the beauty of fracture
—amnesia

I leave the showroom quietly
don't tell him
what it feels like to rise up
off a mattress
and crave the mutism
of your own body

Fragments

I push these tiny bones
around the surface of the table
as it were a shell game

I have pulled out each section of self
unsnapped each from the hinge
placed them here
for examination

I have made a promise
not to take out too many at a time
—I have a fear of losing track
of smaller things, odd shapes

I don't understand how
a false structure holds itself together
in spite of a splintering foundation

I hear voices from another room
hours fall down my legs
I know I am running out of time
before they find me
scattered all over the surface

soon, my time is up
I quickly put everything back in place

the door explodes open
the winds of tyranny
rip through the center of the room
— everything is destroyed

I look down
practicing the same sacraments
of cleaving
rehearsing the same alibis
begging for someone
to say something

but the room is empty

I speak in broken English
to the dark mahogany
who admits nothing

The Day Breaks Off in Uneven Chunks

All day, I think about my mother
standing in the kitchen
in the silence of January
chipping away,
defrosting the freezer
avoiding the Freon tubes
rushing, cursing, rushing
so the food wouldn't go to waste

my sisters hid in their rooms,
but I stood next to her
watching water droplets
form on bags of frozen vegetables
wilting on the counter

I stared at the package of frozen lamb,
the ribs poking out
almost ethereal

in my mind
I reassembled the body
of the lamb
before they pulled the wool away

my mother scolded me
as she worked
"do something useful"

when it was over
I put all the food back in the freezer
carefully, swiftly
while she cleaned the knife

I put the vegetables far to one side
the meat to the other

I pushed the bones back into place
the lamb's

then mine

Rupture

Someone cracks an egg in a bowl
and the world is broken

a silver fork ruptures the yolk,
and the sea is never whole again

an omelette is made
the egg loses itself
among the butter and onion
and shredded cheese

but when it is folded over
just before it leaves the pan
the chef notices something
about the brown edges
—the soft way a crust forms

sooner than expected
everything slides onto a white plate
and the table genuflects

as morning passes
there may be small ways
we remember the shell
times we shudder at the sound
of shattering

but even after the pan
is removed from an open flame
we find graceful ways
to slide out of a room

and clean our plates
in a small kitchen
with no running water

To Someone I Must Forget

There are days
I don't even remember you

there are times
when I leave my pockets
inside out
like a brooding past

I can't recall
the exact way I used to
drop my chin towards the floor
when you came into the room

I can't lay the memories upon the table
as if I could see through paper thin years

the letters I have written
always come back
moist with melancholy
structured by the grit of your hands

I keep wondering why you can't
read this
or turn the page over
look for another answer

I keep wondering what must be said
to make my skin forget
calloused hands against a throat

if I use all those words

bone
salt
knowledge
memory
marrow

will you understand
any better
where you reside

Living Abroad

I want to move
to a country
where everyone speaks
another language

each person
a different dialect
each neighborhood
an unfamiliar terrain

I want to live
in a backhouse
where the gardener
understands why I will not
water the flowers

I want to live at the end
of a dirt road
where the path
has blended into the field

I want to listen
only to the stories of the coyotes
who cry out to me
in the linguistics
of forgotten tongues

I do not want to remember
how love falls away
and blends into the side alleys
of an abandoned city

I don't want to know
that you live half way across town
broken in your Alzheimer's
broken from the decades
we have not spoken

I will close the heavy door tonight
set out on my own
I will wander, like a displaced foreigner
looking for a frail, older woman
who resembles you
who cannot speak my name

1976 YouTube of Nadia Comaneci

I watch the video
over and over
fixate on her thin frame
her small, poised hands

she was 14
I was 14
her body takes flight
above the uneven parallel bars

the first
"perfect ten" score
I sat on the hardwood floor
my legs crossed, pretzel-like,
breakable

in 1976, I too was practicing
floor exercise and
found ways to unfold my body
I learned how to hold myself
in specific postures
found ways to fall, gracefully.

often, I wondered about Romania
I wondered about small rooms
and the way she looked at herself
in the mirror late at night

I watched Nadia
I watched her
I prayed for her safe landing
I kneeled in front of the television set
and ignored the smell of booze
the particular way
it crept under my door at night

I wonder now
if she looks back
does she ponder how she escaped
how a young woman
will cross a border
decades later
knowing she can never return

Travel Guide

When you get there
tell them you know me
tell them
I am the one with the
charred skin

the broken hands

when you pass through the curtain
do not be afraid
fall into the furrows
of your un-forgiven self

speak to them
in the silent language of
a peculiar darkness

I will watch you from the ledge
meandering, mingling
in the land of the dead

you will notice
they don't care
if they are standing or sitting

you will notice
they only care
that you came to visit

keep going, follow the path
of telekinesis
moving yourself secretly
in the chess game
of your own mortality

before you open your eyes
watch the atheist and the sinner
merge into one

and when your husband
taps your shoulder and asks you "what's wrong"
"who are you talking to?"
you can tell him "I don't know"
"I only remember falling."

Exit Here

When you emerge
from the grocery store

the parking lot is empty
the streets vacant
the concrete
has forgotten you

you wonder if this is
the same dream
where you wake and the world
is gone

you wonder if the sky
is actually the roof of your house
and you are fractured
as always
and your pillow is
choking you

you walk for hours
noticing how the trees
bend like battered women

you avoid the hairline fractures
in the sidewalk
hoping they will be spared
by your heavy footsteps

the day dims to nothing
the ruined crows appear
wrap their claws
around the sagging telephone lines
and finally
you run
still escaping your house
as you did in seventh grade
the streets just as barren

the asphalt blessed
in the black of night

When in Doubt

Mark yourself safe
on facebook,
even though the water
is rising

mark yourself safe
so you don't have to explain
why you are drowning
in a dry creek bed

mark yourself as alive
even though you are suffocating
and no one believes you

mark yourself as weary
when you explain
panic attacks
to your new doctor

notice the way
he turns his head
to feign sincerity

show him the claw marks
of the history
inside your body

explain how the
neurotransmitters
have gone haywire
how every organ in you
is a lost grenade

pretend you've escaped the
hurricane
and when you go to sleep at night

tell the truth

mark yourself dead

Vacant

I like leaving my neighborhood
when it is still morning-dark
before the sun incinerates
the subconscious of the soil

I pretend the houses
have never been inhabited

never known the love
that ruins walls

I pass each structure
imagine no one is sleeping
or turning over
while the floor boards breathe

all day
I dream of unfolding myself
inside the narrow hallways

pretend there are confessions
hiding beneath the floor boards

but instead
the paint peels off this cracked day

and I am left standing
in an entry way
that has absolved me
of nothing

Fade In

In a room far off from the main hallway
in front of the mirror
each actor places a painted mask
over their face

they have spent years
with oil based stains
leaking down the backs of their necks

each paper Mache curve
was molded by the hands of a sinner
painted by the prophecy of deep red

they know how to breathe
inside the mask
how to measure the air of atonement

they know their voices sound muffled
when the audience leans forward
and pretends to understand the rehearsed lines

they understand that death
is an understudy

they think that each time they
enter and exit my dreams
that I won't recognize them

but I stand off stage
unseen, not breathing
watching how they sneak
into these perverse scripts

the man who does the lighting
always paralyzed

following the skirted line of velvet robes

each curtain a silence

Back Stage

You are like a stripper
who never takes off her clothes

you speak as if
you have spent your life on stage
but stay fully clothed
behind a dark curtain

on occasion
you perform a tangled dance
barely lift your skirt to onlookers
they never see
your thin shoulder blades
your rib cage that rises and falls
with each breath

you hold your thoughts
like worn dollar bills
dirty — and close to the hip

your scarves
are folded carefully
with the rest of your memories
in a redwood dresser drawer
always off its track

you don't tell anyone
why you sleep in your clothes
why you fold yourself in two places
before bed

how the night enters you

your whole body a fugue

It's No Secret

I understand
you know how to lean
into a woman
how to search inside
her half naked eyes
for affirmation

you think the length
of your stare across a room
is all a goddess needs to hear thunder

you have pressed your tongue
beyond the roof of her mouth
until she feels you
as fluid on the brain

I hear you have held
the lower backs
of whores and women
with floral skirts

each a rosary bead
you have prayed upon

when she kneels before you,
are you merciful
with her open mouth
do you understand the
penance of an open jaw

do you remember
the color of her hair
how swallowing you
may be merely a proclivity
for stretching a tired neck

when the dress falls to the floor
do you notice the cloth
scattered and imperfect

do you notice her hands
the delicate fingers
the bone structure
how they are searching
for a confession

Thursday Night Walk With the Dog

For the third time this week
we walk by the house
where the woman died suddenly
of an aneurism

we pause at the driveway
and the endless concrete
stops us in our path
again

we both notice
a small lamp inside the living room
how it flickers off and on
how the light in a room
disappears like mercy

we should head back home
but don't want to leave
it's as if we could stand forever
and notice
how loss remains open like a gate

Taking a Walk on the Path Behind Our House

Upon entering
I notice a sign that says
"park closes after dusk"
as I approach
the letters fall off
break upon impact

bicyclists pass
ignore me

as I head for home
I drop my sins
like acorns upon the trail
as the darkness grows jealous
of the hell bent sky

a small branch
from a sycamore is bending
and falls
in the creek bed

only the twigs understand
this particular sound
— how a tree is never the same
after autumn

All this Talk

Why all this talk of sky
all this looking up

the proverbial straining of the neck
all this murmur of sacred shades of blue

why all the reaching up
for Orion
and the repentant moon

the grasping
the stories that lie like throw pillows
atop faded clouds

the light years of your distant truth
filtering down to earth

where you take a shower in a dark room
where you wash dusk
from your hair

the pockets of ancient azure
never knowing
of your morning rage
the thud of the body
when it falls

it is the rich, steadfast ground
that receives you
after you fall
holds you,
until someone finds you

it is the sacrament of salt and soil
that make a place
in the bent blades of grass

Ornithology

I want to freelance
in the eve of birds

not fly, or soar
or carry the strength of wind

I want to know
how to find the thin power lines
how to balance
when the flock
leaves you behind

how to identify
the noises of departure

I want to know
how to find the distance
from branch to soil
how to atone
for the loss of gravity

I want to learn
to become an unencumbered silence
and extract autumn
from each weary leaf

I want to be a statue-like
in the depleted dawn

I want you to understand
why I bathe myself
in the ruined twilight

Raven in Flight

The sky has never forgiven you
for your blackness

when you fly
inside the backdrop of night
I am the only one who sees you

you claw your way
into my dreams
but I cannot
find you in the morning

your beak weighs heavy
on the ruined dusk
I hear your guttural call
when I am running
down to the dry river bed

I remember the same way
you flew over me
when I was running away
in second grade

how you knew my mother
would find me
how you have
pulled away at the skin
of my regret

years have passed and still
you land at random
on the uneven fence
of silence

always helping me
to understand
what it means to
live as the heretic

to realize
there is no contrition
in the fading light

As the Week Goes By

I am looking for
your obituary

not the one in the paper
that will give your
birth and death dates
nor the one
that lists the paragraphs of your life

I am looking
for the one
I wrote in my hand
decades ago

the one where I was
banished from the house
when I took all my school
projects and pictures
and my own bruised
flesh

the one that
shows the burial
of a young woman
in my own clothing
reading her own eulogy

everyone is gathering
at the grave site
but me

after all
a black sheep
has her wool to groom
in the hour of your death

The Burial was Wednesday

Everyone gathered
at your grave site
but me

when I think of you
in the casket
I can't imagine
how a body
can be any darker

so instead
I wonder
what prayers were
muttered
what psalm
they all believe
will deliver you
from evil

"though I walk through the valley
of the shadow of death"

but here I am
walking away
dragging my own corpse
across a desolate valley

wearing the cloak
of the heretic
making sure the
fabric doesn't unravel

I tell myself I'm ready
for exile
I find kindling
build a small
familiar camp fire

and listen for the sound
of breaking twigs
in the distance

Looking for the Father's name

I go to the cemetery
two weeks
after the memorial service

I go alone

I notice
where the grass
has been tamped down
methodically
around the burial site

I wonder if
your crimes
might
creep back up
to find their way
through the cracks
in the ground

as if your sins
are no longer

as if
I can forget
your cold hands
after midnight

as if you never said
"I didn't do anything
to those girls they didn't want"

I head back to the car
I hear the earth groan
as if it too
knows
how painful it is
to hold you
inside itself

For All of Us Who

It was my brother, it was my uncle, I was alone, someone was in the next room, it was my father, I young, I was in third grade, I was in college, I knew him, I didn't know him, he put something in my drink, I was wearing winter clothes, I wasn't wearing any clothes, I was on my way to work, I was on my way home, I was afraid of him, he told me he would fire me, he told me he would kill me, he told me to shut up or he'd take the kids, he told me I was a whore, he told me I teased him, he told me I would ruin the family, he told me no one would believe me, he said nothing and stared through me until I was dead, I didn't tell for years, I told and was not believed, I have never told, I have bad dreams, I avoid parties, I avoid dark rooms, I avoid long lurking glances, I avoid skirts, or winter or summer or seasons where my skin remembers violation. I drink, I don't eat, I keep it quiet, I tell my friends, I take pills, I don't walk alone at night, I hold my lover's hand, I worry too much about my kids, I need to tell the truth.

I

need

to

tell

the

truth

Coastal College Town

I leave the hotel room early
looking for a small café
my husband still in bed,
the sheets half off

I merge onto the same freeway
of thirty years ago
the same one who took me
away from home

I am wondering
again
if I got everything from the garage,
the sheets from the closet,
the letters you stole from me,
pictures of myself in grade school

I knew I would never return
you knew it too

the fog breaks
I find a place where the locals go
on my way out
throw a dollar in the tip jar

on the way back to the hotel
I find a hidden easement
between the small beach cottages

I find a few narrow steps
each slightly covered with sand
each, a geology of fine gravel and salient sorrow

I think
I did get everything

I think mostly about the sorcery of the word
"whore"
your voice low and moist in the back of my ear

how every day
decades later
I am thankful for small easements,
how the fog suddenly lifts itself from an old road

How to Watch a Bird Die

Take the dog out
early in the morning
notice the same Eucalyptus
how the crow is
still perched
half frozen
on the same mid-point
of the tree

notice how the claws are stuck
and how the back of your neck
seems damp
and full of sunlight
all at once

each day
tell yourself " it will be over soon"

tell yourself
that's just the way nature works
tell yourself
it's intrusive to do anything else

urge the dog to walk closer to you
instead of pulling
pulling you back to the tree
over and over

remind yourself
you have to get back and
make breakfast

imagine how peaceful
a bird looks
when it is finally
melting into the dirt

imagine
the ground is atonement
and the murder of crows
just taking flight
are finally free of sin

Infatuation

I am in love with silence
the way it can fracture a room

how it moves across the stairway
through you
as if you wore the wrong dress

I step in and out of the false quiet
as if it is a kept woman
as if it understands the agreements of
entrance and exit

I hold its hand, only when convenient
only behind the champagne table
when no one else is looking

I act as if the wooden beams of the ceiling
are not falling

I pretend this room was not
built on a fault line
I pretend the plates of language
have not slipped like a loose jaw bone

and I am not standing here
bracing myself
in a doorway
already collapsing

Strands

The next time I wash my hair
I will be old
there will be no place
for the strands to fall

years will have passed through
me
and I will not understand
the knots
the cutting away

the next time I fold my hands
there will be winter
falling through them

I will look over my shoulder —
old leaves
will have fallen
over my grave

I will rinse my mouth
with my own sins
and as my teeth fall out,
the coarse tongue
of loss will recede

my bones
will nod
grateful to the broken earth
as it scatters itself
inside my veins

Become

Find your place in the river
the smooth stone

find places to open your mouth
where the salmon sing
in the chorus of returning

find the widest edge
where the soil seeks atonement

find the underground
where the coldest winters
break the land
like offered bread

find the side stream
where night can no longer exist
where darkness becomes an edge
unto itself

become the sound
of a rushing current
in the crisp dawn

stand as atheist to the
flat land

live in rebellion
careening with the white water

writhe until
the migration ends

Omen

For three years
the black squirrel
visits our backyard

I say I hate it,
"it doesn't look right"
I read in science magazines
that it's a mutation
a normal occurrence in nature
but every day
I think it is a bad omen
every day
I encourage the dogs
to run after him

I watch his whirling
curling
ascent up the tree
I find relief
as he moves away from me
into the next yard

winter passes through me
a close friend my age
dies of a brain tumor
I do not wear black to the funeral

later that week
I step outside
in mid afternoon
and see the black squirrel sitting
quietly by our pond

our eyes meet
and for that split second
I see how I have banished
the secret body
within the body

I see his small heart pulsing
how sorrow fills a cavern
and keeps beating

Acknowledgments

Grateful acknowledgements to the following publications in which these poems first appeared:

Atticus Review: "Infatuation"

The Big Muddy: "Solstice"

Bird as Black as the Sun: "Raven in Flight"

Blue Fifth Review: "All This Talk"

Chabot Review: "Fragments"

Collateral Damage: "For All of Us Who"

Comstock Review: "Fault Lines", "Crumbling", "Four Miles from the Center of Town", "Shadow Light", "Burn", "Looking for the Father's Name"

Crab Creek Review: "Hula Hoop Turns 50", "Gardening" (Crab Creek Review Poetry Award 2016)

I-70 Review: "Ornithology"

Ina Coolbrith Anthology: "Flash Flood"

Iodine Poetry Journal: "Curvature of the Spine"

Kentucky Review: "The Night Before Surgery"

Mocking Heart Review: "Feast", "Silences"

Oberon: "MRI", "Thursday Night Walk with the Dog"

Pirene's Fountain: "Rupture", "Fade In", "Back Stage"

Porter Gulch Review: "After Winter", "Aisle Five, Sheets and Linens"

Prick of the Spindle: "Strands"

River Styx: "1976 You Tube of Nadia Comaneci"

RiverSedge: "How to Sort the Living from the Dead"

Spoon River Poetry Review: "Travel Guide"

The Stray Branch: "Accessory After the Fact", "Catatonic Walk While The Sun Drops Out of the Sky", "Exit Here"

Third Wednesday: "Omen"

Two Bridges Review: "Lent", "Prime Meridian"

Valparaiso Poetry Review: "How to Watch a Bird Die"

Thank you to the following people for helping this manuscript become a book. For supporting my poems or reading the manuscript, offering advice and helping me put this book forth into the world.

My daughter Erika Post, my husband Kevin Gunn, and to poets David Alpaugh, Lynne Knight, Francesca Bell, and Erica Goss.

I offer gratitude to each of you for your time, attention, energy and belief in my poems.

About the Author

Connie Post served as the first Poet Laureate of Livermore from 2005 to 2009. During that time she wrote over twenty five poems of occasion for civic events. She also created two popular reading series. Post's poems appear widely in magazines, such as Calyx, Dogwood, Blue Fifth Review, Two Bridges Review, Comstock Review, Spoon River Poetry Review, River Styx, Crab Creek Review, Slipstream, One, The Big Muddy, Slippery Elm, Valparaiso Poetry Review and Verse Daily. Her first full length collection, *Floodwater*, was published in 2014 by Glass Lyre Press and won the Lyrebird Award. Her chapbook And When the Sun Drops won the 2012 Aurorean Editor's chapbook prize. Her work has appeared in several anthologies, including Alongside we Travel - Contemporary Poets on Autism (NYQ Books, 2019), Collateral Damage and Carrying the Branch (Glass Lyre Press,) and Truth to Power Writers Respond To The Rhetoric Of Hate And Fear (Cutthroat Magazine).

Her poetry awards include the 2018 Liakoura Award, the Crab Creek Review Poetry Award, the Caesura Award, and the Prick of the Spindle Poetry Competition. In addition, she won second place for the Jack Kerouac Poetry Prize and the Atticus Review Poetry Prize.

Glass Lyre Press

exceptional works to replenish the spirit

Glass Lyre Press is an independent literary publisher interested in technically accomplished, stylistically distinct, and original work. Glass Lyre seeks diverse writers that possess a dynamic aesthetic and an ability to emotionally and intellectually engage a wide audience of readers.

Glass Lyre's vision is to connect the world through language and art. We hope to expand the scope of poetry and short fiction for the general reader through exceptionally well-written books, which evoke emotion, provide insight, and resonate with the human spirit.

Poetry Collections
Poetry Chapbooks
Select Short & Flash Fiction
Anthologies

www.GlassLyrePress.com

www.ingramcontent.com/pod-product-compliance
Lightning Source LLC
Chambersburg PA
CBHW030350100526
44592CB00010B/892